Sponsor's Name:

Phone:

Email:

# The Ultimate Napkin Presentation

## Explode Your Network Marketing Business

# "The Coding Bonus"

John Alexander

John Alexander

Copyright © 2010 John Alexander

2nd Edition 2019

All rights reserved.

ISBN-13: 978-1499343953

ISBN-10: 1499343957COPYRIGHT

ALL RIGHTS RESERVED. No part of this book may be reproduced or transmitted for resale or use by any party other than the individual purchaser who is the sole authorized user of this information. All other reproduction or transmission, in any form or by any means, electronic or mechanical, including photocopying, recording or by any informational storage or retrieval method, is prohibited without express written permission from John Alexander.

# Introduction

You hold in your hands a Powerful System that will <u>Explode your Monthly Income and your Downline Business Organization.</u>

You are about to learn how this powerful tool (this book) can change your financial future.

Multi-million dollar income is a proven fact in network marketing. The Ultimate Wealth System reveals secret key ingredients of DUPLICATION.

You will NOT have to :

- BEG others to join the business
- SELL unwanted products/services to anyone
- TALK to anyone not interested in joining your business
- CHASE friends and family

Let this Book do the heavy lifting for you.

## The Goal

Self-generating income is the type of income everyone strives to attain. Imagine not being tied to a day-to-day grind of specific work hours to assure your income. Self-generating income is income that streams in without your daily or even monthly effort.

*Now that's powerful! **That's network marketing! It's building an organization that generates income to you whether you continue to work at it or you retire. A self-generating residual income.***

## The Basics

Read each short section and study the NAPKIN illustrations which will demonstrate how using this system in your network marketing business can create wealth for you and your team, beyond your wildest comprehension.

The goal of a network marketer is the exponential growth of their organization in the shortest time possible and product sales. Commissions and residual income grow and multiply over and over again as your organization grows.

# When to Introduce this Book to your Client/Prospect

Timing is important when using a tool like this. This isn't usually given to a client until after you have gone through two phases first. The reason for this is that the "money" aspect of a new business is not the ever the "real" reason someone gets involved with starting a new business.

Rather, money is a tool that makes their real reason for joining come true. Their real reason for starting a business will be revealed in phase one. Your company often has that part built into their opportunity presentation, but it will still be your job to make sure that is fully addressed before moving on to the "money and income" phase.

Phase one in the joining process will answer and focus on your client's "WHY." Why are they looking at starting a business or needing/wanting more income. Once that is determined, then and only then is someone open to learning about how the money (earning) part works and can benefit them.

Don't put money before their true needs and desires. Needs and desires look like the following, a closer relationship with their spouse, security for their family, ending the thought of what happens if I can't make the rent/mortgage payment, dreams of moving up, helping their charity more, freedom from a job they hate, a retirement account or college fund for their kids, on and on. Money is the tool that gets them their needs and desires, therefore money isn't their true desire and dream.

Once they, and you, know their true desires, then the conversation can turn to HOW to make those dreams and desires come true, and there is only one way, making more money.

## The Ultimate Napkin Presentation

As in any business, income builds over time, as you grow and develop your business. In a network marketing business, you may start by earning a profit of say, $100.00 a month and before you know it, that $100.00 is now $5,000.00 a month, as more time and more growth occurs, $20,000, $50,000, even $100,000 a month can be possible just as it has for some of our top people in our company. Now this doesn't mean that just because they made those amounts that you will. Only you can determine your income by the efforts you put into your business, but also don't let anyone's income limited you either, you may have what it takes to even exceed them. That's how business works, it releases limitations on income. Jobs have limitations but owning your own business has NO Limitation. Many people in this industry, over time, have and continue to develop, monthly incomes equal to Fortune 500 CEO income levels.

We've looked at your true desires, your true goals you want achieved by owning your own business, now lets look at how that happens in the one business type that allows you to harness your own business organization's efforts. As they grow their income in pursuit of their dreams and desires, it automatically grows your income, making your dreams and desires come true.

$100,000

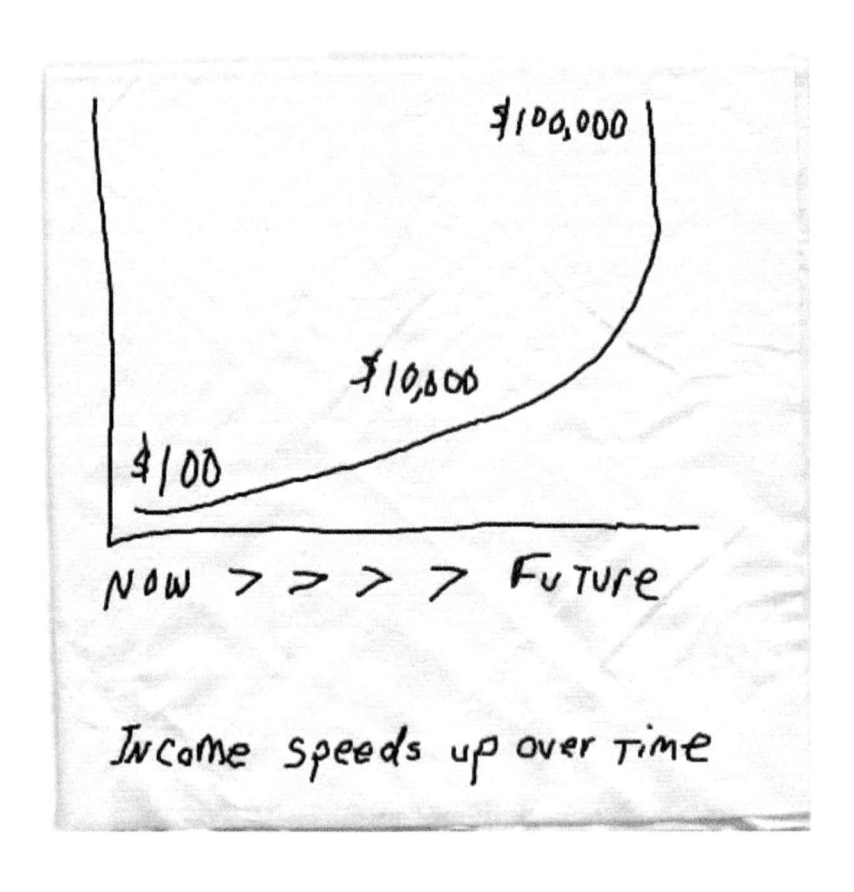

$10,000

$100

NOW > > > > Future

Income speeds up over time

## Your goal is to BUILD... it's not to Sell!

Emphasis must be placed on building your organization first (the distribution organization). Product sales will follow the natural path of growth from the distributors (your downline).

## *LEARN YOUR PRODUCT, BUT DON'T FOCUS ON SELLING YOUR PRODUCT ...* Get it right by learning the correct order of how to create your network marketing business.

The mistake most new networkers make is they think they need to sell a lot of their product and from products sales, their organization will grow and develop. That would have been like a young Steve Jobs selling his new invention, the personal computer, to a few computer nerds and expecting them to sell the computer to the world. That's not how he did it, that's not how any business is grown successfully.

Remember, the first order of business is to BUILD your business structure. When Steve Jobs first started Apple Computer, he first created the product, the personal computer, then he immediately started building his distribution system for that product. He knew he couldn't personally sell enough computers to get to his goal. He recruited others to do that for him. People whose job was to sell computers, not just use them. A successful network marketer builds their organization and understands the natural outcome is that sales will follow. It is very important to place your energy onto the correct path to create the momentum that gives you the best chance to succeed. Steve Jobs knew he needed a team to build his dream. Let's follow Steve Job's example on growing your organization.

*Your true customer is a person that wants to start a home-based business. And needs help doing it!*

A successful networker understands the business they are in and understands that networking is how the business is built.

This is how successful people in your company were able to build their organization to hundreds or thousands of other networkers, many in just months, some over a few short years.

This kind of organization building translates into a fortune in commissions and bonuses, that keep coming in even when you are asleep or on vacation. It's a cash producing machine, that doesn't sleep or goes on vacation!

**Duplicate** and then there were many ...

## The Original King of "Systems"

The creator of McDonald's restaurant, Ray Kroc understood the correct order of launching his business successfully. His business was not selling hamburgers to the public, his business was recruiting others to sell hamburgers to the public, called Franchisees (restaurant owners). He had great tools to help recruit his business owners. One of his best tools made it easy to duplicated how the food was prepared.

## Ray Kroc's Secret

He made it so simple that any 16 year-old is able to produce anything on the menu; cooked exactly the same way time-after-time. It made it easy for franchisees to hire and train unskilled workers to run the "product and sales" part of the business. This allowed massive duplication and growth of McDonalds.

McDonald's success makes clear why the ==duplication of a system must be efficient and easy to utilize.== We are all aware, even today how many such systems generate wealth day after day, month after month, year after year.

As a network marketer you will use a similar, efficient duplicating system to introduce the business and train new team members. Remember, this is accomplished with a minimum of time investment which adds to the simplicity of the system for the next person to duplicate.

## Tools and how History repeats itself...

Historically, network marketing has used the latest communication technology available at the time to carry out the duplication process. In the 1990's, cassette tapes, VHS, video tapes and fax-on-demand were used by hundreds of thousands of networkers to train and duplicate their organization.

Today, it's conference calls, webcasts, DVD's, online videos, E-books and E-mail, funnels, and social media.. There are also mainstay methods which have changed little since the 1970's and that is mainly the live event or live meetings, live training sessions and periodic conventions held by leaders and the Company for its members. Even if you are using online and other automated methods to grow your business, you will always want to include live face to face connection with your people. This often comes in the form of your company's national meetings. There is nothing more powerful and moving that will get you and your team charged up and producing more and growing faster than investing in the time to go to those live events. Magic happens there and if you are not there, you are missing out on many levels of your business that can't always be explained in words.

In our ever-changing world time is a precious commodity and you will encounter most new team members prefer a time efficient method to build their network marketing business.

As a multi-billion dollar industry, network marketing dominates the home-based business industry. More people start their own business inside an Network Marketing Company than any other way. And for good reason. It works, the product has already been created and the sales have been proven. And right now, one of the easiest ways to grow your business is using social media to find other people wanting some of the same goals and desires you want. Still keep in mind that social media is a distribution method and is not a replacement for one-on-one contact and relationship building. Use social media to sort, and one-on-one to develop team members.

# How to Introduce Your Opportunity to Others

This BOOK as a primary tool will place you in a win-win situation and begin to grow your organization.

Remember, never, ever HARD SALE people into your organization. If you have to hard sell, they realize that they too have to hard sell and most people can't, won't, and shouldn't hard sell anyone. We want them pushing us, not us pulling them.

This book will introduce prospects to the network marketing concept and the **power of duplication using your company's Coding Bonus.** If after they have listened to your company's presentation and they still are fence sitting. Get this book into their hands and ask that they read it and let's have a final conversation where you tell me if this is right for you or not right for you.

What you do and say in the early stages of introducing the business to someone is being observed by your new person. Therefore, you will need to limit the "talking" to a minimum and not attempt to sell your prospect on your product or service. Otherwise, they will feel they must do the same thing.

The process of introducing a prospect to a home-based business in network marketing should begin by establishing a desire for earning more income. Fortunately, this process can be done quickly using just a few questions.

## Your Simple Introduction Script

It's easy to turn almost any conversation to one discussing today's economy, which can lead you to say...

1. "My industry is exploding right now and so I'm expanding my own business. Do you know of anyone that may want to earn some extra money?"

Phrasing the question in this manner usually allows them to volunteer their own interest and opens the door for this next question.

2. "Are you looking for part-time or full-time type income?"

3. Why are you looking to earn more income?

4. How would that change your life if that could happen?

5. **I have a way that could make that happen if you are truly serious about wanting that for yourself. Is it important enough to spend 30 minutes in learning how it might be possible for you to do just that?**

At this point, guide them to your company's live conference call or online business presentation, . Everyone can see how this makes the process possible to duplicate by almost anyone. And more importantly, they see themselves coping the process with the same success.

# The Tool

**This Book ...** is an amazing tool which creates a duplicated system for the successful networker.

**This Book ...** is an effective teaching tool for a new person learning the core concepts of network marketing because it simplifies the introduction process of network marketing to others.

**This Book** demonstrates why there is minimal time invested for all parties involved.

**Key points ...**

Let this book do the work for you. In the early stages of introducing the network marketing business to a new person, remember they are observing you. They are asking themselves if they can "duplicate" what you are saying and doing.

Simplicity is key and this book provides you with a simple but valuable tool which also aids in breaking the ice.

So DON'T SELL, Don't give details, no matter what they ask!

Your job is to get them to your Company's Business Opportunity Call or Presentation, nothing else.

## So Who Sells the Products?

Your company or upline will provide you with online/conference call presentations which will be available at the appropriate time for your prospect to listen to and learn more about the product and compensation plan.

Your company sells the products, they do customer support. Don't do their job because they won't and can't do your job. Yes, of course you will use and talk about your experience with your company's products/services, but don't focus your business on selling as much as on building.

Sales come as you build. You can of course do it the slow way and Sell as you build, and for some that may be they way they are comfortable doing it, but selling is best left to the customer, they can buy want they feel they need and your company has already built the system online for them to find and order what they want.

*Today, Websites Sell products, Not You!*

## The Importance of the Napkin Presentation

Using this book as a primary tool is important in the timing of your introduction of network marketing to a new person. It is very important they read the book at a point in their joining your business because they should understand the concept of "The Napkin Presentation."

In recent years, "The Napkin Presentation" has been utilized aggressively by network marketers to teach the basic concept of the power of duplication in their perspective Companies.

The napkin presentation simplifies an idea or method because it is used as a visual aid. A napkin illustration drives important points clearly and easily.

## Let the Tools do the work for you because...

Using this book as your "Napkin Presentation" takes the work out of it and makes it more time efficient. So no, you don't actually use real napkins to do a napkin presentation, it's just the idea of conveying concepts so simple, they could be explained on a napkin.

This book does the napkin presentation for you.

*A one-on-one napkin presentation can take a considerable amount of time.*

And remember, the new person will be able to duplicate this method when introducing network marketing to their new people.

**So how does "The Napkin Presentation" demonstrate the power of network marketing with financial gain?**

## Two Ways to Build

1. Larger profits are gained by building your team deep rather than wide.
2. Building deep insures your downline will continue to duplicate and your organization grows on its own.

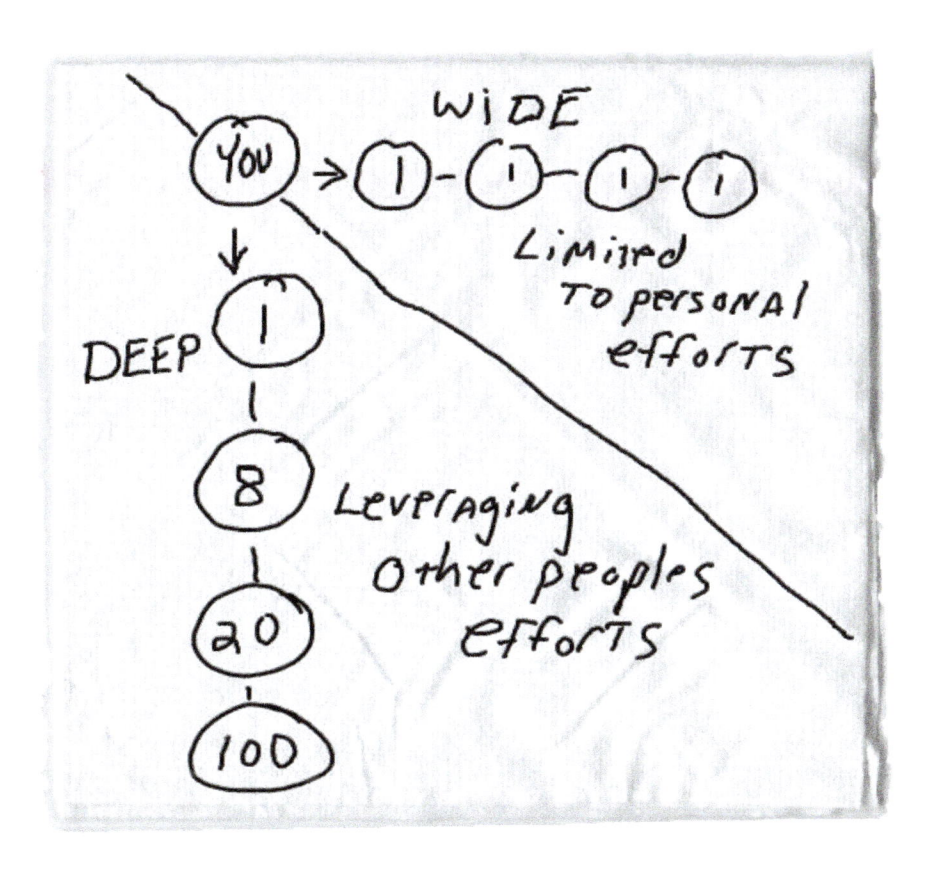

```
         WIDE
(YOU) → (1)-(1)-(1)-(1)
  ↓              Limited
DEEP (1)         to personal
      |          efforts
     (8)   Leveraging
      |    other peoples
     (20)  efforts
      |
     (100)
```

## Where the Real Money is Earned… The "Bonus"

The "Bonus Payment":

*What is a bonus?  A "Bonus" is a set amount paid to you one time, when someone joins your almost anywhere in your downline.  It goes by names like "Coding Bonus, Leadership Bonus, etc"*

A strong compensation plan always includes a bonus payment that pays between $10 and $100 or more to everyone that enters your downline, to unlimited levels below you. This is an important factor in your research of which company is right for you, as some will restrict their bonuses to 1 or 2 levels. You want a company that provides "unlimited level" bonuses.

Let's examine how these bonuses can build a your organization and your income at the same time.  By the way, we will not actually look at all the other ways your company pays you, so yes, you will earn other ways, but the coding bonus is the main driving source of income over time and for maintaining income from the work of others in your business, rather than your own efforts.

The Ultimate Wealth System

In our first example, we will use a single person to demonstrate how bonuses work.

This Napkin demonstrates "building deep"

- You sponsor one person and teach that person how to sponsor one person and they do the same for 2 more levels deep.

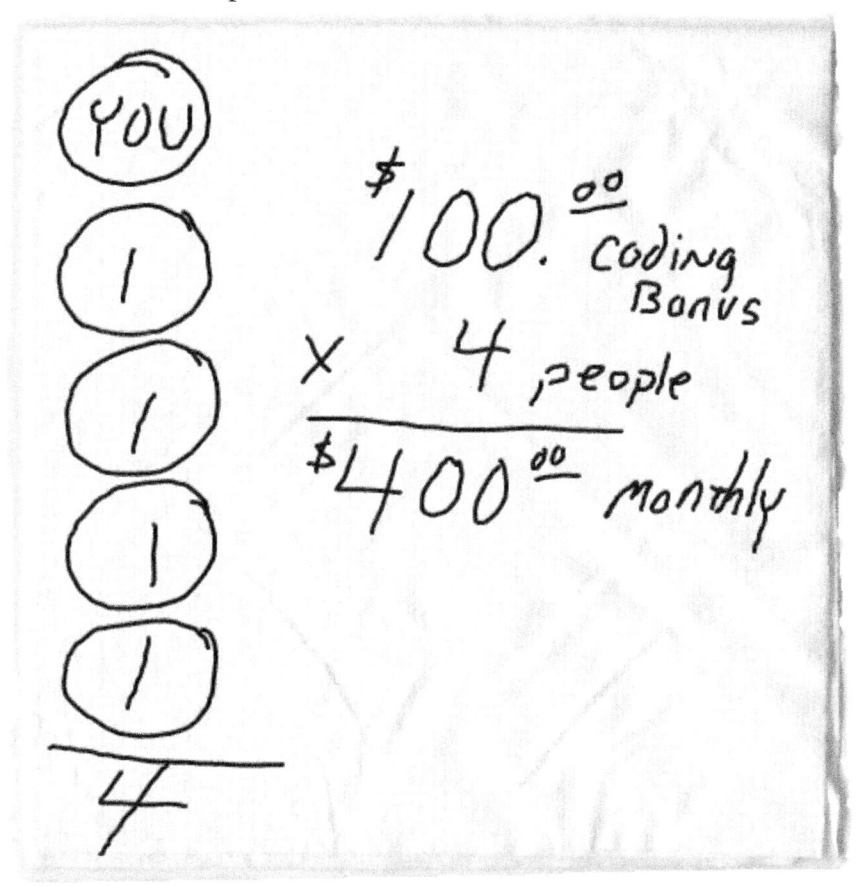

*(Napkin illustration: YOU with 4 levels of 1 person each, totaling 4)*

$100.00 Coding Bonus
× 4 people
$400.00 monthly

Observe the illustration showing 4 people in your total

25

organization.

Example of how bonuses add up:

A bonus that pays $100.00 where you have 4 people in your downline you would earn you $400.00 … $100 per person (4 x 100).

$400 is earned because you have 4 people in your downline that joined your organization. You don't have to sponsor everyone personally to earn bonuses.

## Now… Let's get Real!

The next napkin shows what real life starts to look like. The fact is that not every one that joins your organization will be ready to start at that exact moment, life gets in the way sometimes, or your newest person may not be up to speed yet on how to work the business. Some will even quit when the next shiny object shows up in their inbox or on their Facebook news feed. So let's just stick with some really small numbers and see why those numbers are more "real life" numbers that can be achieved; and then what those numbers can ultimately produce in revenue over time.

Let's look at what someone might expect if they are working the business to some degree yet not absolutely killing it yet. There is plenty of room for improvement as your team get better at sponsoring

The Ultimate Wealth System

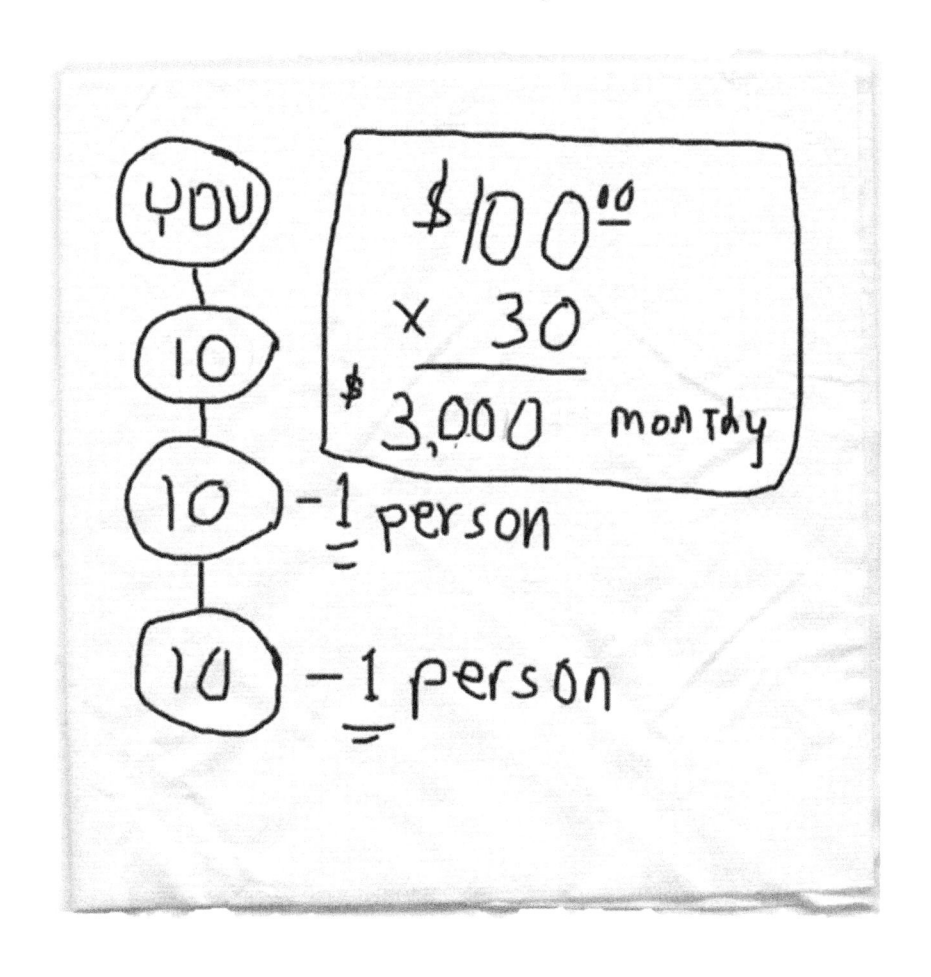

```
(YOU)        $100⁰⁰
  |
 (10)        ×  30
  |         ─────────
 (10) -1    $ 3,000  monthly
      ─ person
      =
 (10) -1 person
      ─
      =
```

1. The first level just below YOU shows 10 people that over time We will assume you have risen in your organization and earning at a $100 coding bonus)

2. This is where real life starts to come in we mentioned at the beginning of this section. Not all 10 people will get the level of also sponsoring 10 each like you do. But at some point we can expect that at least one

person duplicates your methods and reaches the level you achieved then we can assume they begin sponsoring 10 (on avg) a month like you do.

3. And below them, it shows that out of their ten people each month, what if only also steps up to that level of production. The monthly income from just the coding bonus will pay you $3,000 monthly in ongoing revenues. We create machines and machines produce profits month after month. We are still not even looking at the possibility of more than one of each of the ten you sponsor and any of those below them may sponsore at these levels.

This is the amazing effect the coding bonus when used in an online sponsoring machine.

This is the power of duplication in network marketing and why this book is to be used as a primary tool. It is this concept that a new network marketer can better understand through visual aid and be able to act upon. The idea of **Building** the business as the first priority becomes clear by understanding this concept. It illustrates how the Coding Bonus adds up very quickly.

## Let's now zoom out a year in the future?

What do you think your organization will look like in a year if you keep sponsoring at least 10 people a month and some of those do the same?

How many levels down do you think you might be at by then?

How many people in your downline are using your system to produce the same 10 people monthly?

Let's look!

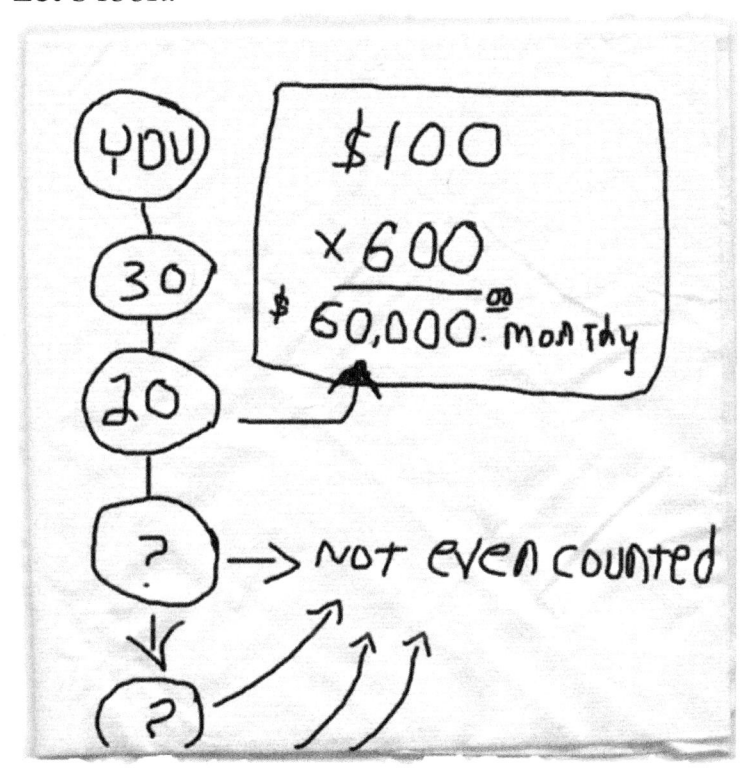

```
YOU
 |
(30)
 |
(10) ────┐   $100
 |       │  × 600
(?) ──→ Not even counted
 ↓       │  $60,000.⁰⁰ monthly
(?)
```

30 people you sponsored doing the same as you would equal 300 people per month coming into your downline and you

Keep in mind we have focused on the Bonuses but you also earn commissions and residuals in this growing organization that pay you month after month as these people make monthly purchases of product/services.

## Power of the Bonus

It is imperative that you find a network marketing company that pays a bonus in order to take advantage of this kind of payment structure from the levels below you.

Look what happens just taking it one more level <u>DEEP</u> …

## Start and Don't Stop Building your Business

As with any business it is realistic to understand that big money is not accomplished overnight. Consistent effort will draw the go-getters to your organization and in turn this will make your downline explode. Most people never succeed in business because they stop at the first signs of failure or a defeat. They also jump from one opportunity to the next. Resist all these "normal" reasons that stop your from building your business. Focus and commit to doing exactly what your sponsor is teaching you to do. You wouldn't be talking to your sponsor if there were not doing something RIGHT. Learn THAT! Duplicate THAT!

While we only demonstrated going down limited levels deep, a good company will pay bonuses to an unlimited depth, meaning the numbers can get staggering.

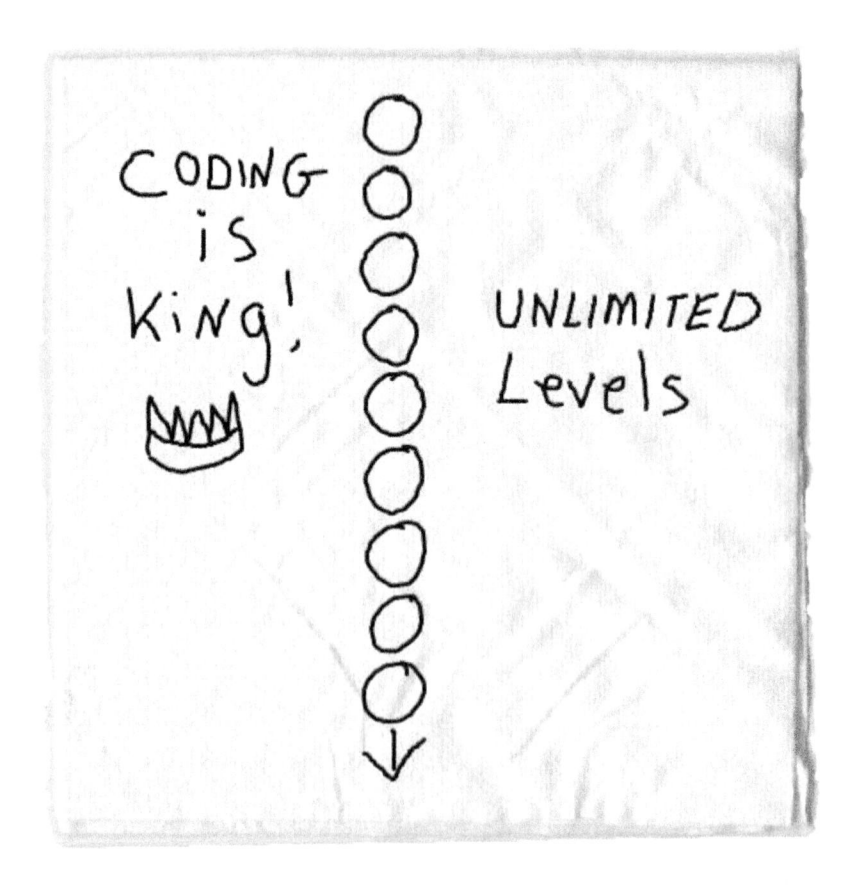

*CODING IS KING!*

*UNLIMITED Levels*

Think about it and ask yourself "How many businesses would

pay me this kind of money even after working for many years?"

**Key points to remember:**
- Stay committed, consistent and focused on BUILDING your team.
- Keep your team focused on building deep first and wide second.
- Use this book as a tool. The work is already done for you.

## GenX & Baby Boomers are the Major Consumer of Products and Services!

Over the next 5 to 15 years, the Baby Boomer Generation and Generation X will be moving into network marketing at a faster pace than ever before in American history.

These two generations control the majority of the buying dollar in America with the baby boomer generation controlling 70% of the wealth and making up 79 million in population numbers.

These two generations will continue to control the wealth in America for the next 30 years. What these two generations want, what interests them, and what they need, determines what they do with their buying/investing dollars. Getting in front of what they want is the way fortunes are made.

Gerber Baby food sales exploded in the 50's and 60's, as the baby boomers were taking their first bites of food. Next, Kenny Shoes sales exploded as they the boomers went off to school. When they started dating in the 1970's, "High Karate" cologne for boys and "Charlie" perfume for girls became giant corporations. On and on it goes. If you cater to the Boomers wants and desires, you can't go wrong.

Ask yourself WHAT DO THEY NEED? WHAT DO THEY WANT? And finally does your company deliver those products and services? If the answer is YES, and they have a Coding Bonus, you have found your own perfect storm of income.

The stock market and real estate has taken its toll on these generations. Many of them are retiring out of the job market or changing jobs, often in hopes of securing significant financial earnings.

Today, they are much more cautious where they put their money and no longer desire to risk capital on large investment opportunities. Yet, they must supplement their income by owning their own home-based business and they know that today's business must be tied to the Internet in some way.

Baby Boomers also have a comfort level with a large corporate entity as most of them worked in that environment during their career.

Gen-X is still employed by corporations but they understand their future is not long term. Network marketing corporations are large companies and give that corporate feel both generations desire, along with a small investment as the risk factor.

Baby Boomers and Generation X are starting to position themselves into network marketing now and they will be the leaders and experts in the industry tomorrow. The Gold Rush is happening NOW!

USE THIS BOOK LIKE A BUSINESS CARD AS WELL!

People throw away or lose business cards, there is simply little value in business cards. But by writing in your contact info on the front page and last page of this book accomplishes both giving Value and Your Contact information in a vehicle they will keep and can always find easily. They may even pull it out later and if you are still at that number and still in a coding company, they may well be ready then. Lastly, we also have this as an Kindle Book allowing you to Gift it to your person Simply find the Kindle version on Amazon. Then click the "Give as Gift" button. You can choose to e-mail the e-book gift to the recipient with a future delivery date, or print out a voucher (which you can then place in a greeting card).

*Call Your Sponsor NOW!!*

| |
|---|
| Sponsor's Name: |
| Phone: |
| Email: |

## So What is Your Next Step?

Call the person who referred this book to you, they will be your sponsor {above} into owning your own successful home based business. Fulfill your financial destiny. The time is NOW!

## ABOUT THE AUTHOR

John Alexander, the creator of the Ultimate Napkin Presentation built a personal downline of over 20,000 people. He has been teaching people nationwide on how to become wealthy in their own home-based business since 1994. John has taught hundreds of thousands across America. He has won numerous awards in the network marketing industry including the top sponsor in more than one network marketing company. Today, John coaches real estate investors, network marketers, and business owners in building and scaling their businesses.

Printed in Great Britain
by Amazon